Ten Mistakes A Manager Should Avoid

Aditi Chopra

DEDICATION

I dedicate this book to two excellent managers with whom I have had the pleasure to work, **Dave Lowry** and **Joe Basil**. I have learned a great deal from both of them. They have also helped shape my career quite a bit.

Preface

I would love to think that I am a born leader. Alas, that is not the case. Like some of my peers, I may have innate leadership qualities and the skill to lead people but leadership skills are quite often learned. A good leader is always learning and that is how she continues to improve and hone in on her leadership skills. In fact, experts claim there is no one perfect leadership style. There are various ways of leading and one should apply the style that suits the circumstances. A seasoned leader will have more than one style of leadership and applies the appropriate style to the situation at hand.

When I took on a management role in my career, I learned a lot on the job. I learned by watching people. I learned by making my own mistakes. Sometimes I learned what I should do by watching people. Sometimes I learned what I should not do by watching other people make mistakes. You don't always learn from what people do right, you also learn from what people don't do right.

Managing people is not just a career, it is a rewarding career! As a manager, you get the chance to shape others' careers and that can be a satisfying experience for you and them. Leadership skills are very important for those who are managing people. A good manager is someone who displays qualities that others want to emulate and follow. People follow a true leader without any obligation or pressure. They follow a good leader because they want to.

I was motivated to write this book so I could share my practical experience with all the budding managers. My hope is that by reading this book, managers will avoid making some mistakes in their leadership career. This book is not a tell-all about leadership. The purpose of this book is to help people avoid making mistakes that could be detrimental to their leadership career.

Aditi Chopra

CONTENTS

1 MICRO-MANAGING

The number one mistake budding managers make is not delegating enough. This often happens when an individual contributor is promoted to become manager of a team he was part of. The transition from being a hands-on individual contributor to becoming a manager is hard. For these individuals, delegation doesn't come naturally.

I still remember the day I was promoted from within the team to take on the role of a manager. For the first few weeks, I was participating in software code review of each code change. Old habits die hard. I was checking each and every line of software code just as I did when I was working as an engineer. I was participating in design and functional reviews and would actually take time to provide my own technical feedback. However, very quickly I realized that if I were to continue the tasks of an engineer as well as take the responsibility of managing the team, 24 hours in a day would not be enough to do everything. Crunch of time forced me to start delegating.

But truly speaking I should have been delegating long before that point. Delegating tasks to your employees is a concept similar to letting go with your children. It is a matter of trusting the employees to take care of tasks assigned to them. But it doesn't come naturally. As a manager, one has to work hard to master this skill and start delegating. Building trust with your team takes time too. Start of delegation has to come from the manager by practicing letting go.

Another mistake new managers often unknowingly make is they tend to micro-manage their teams. If you are a seasoned manager and you are still micro managing, there is something wrong with the picture. However, most if not all new managers tend to micro-manage. This is natural since they are new to the role of a manager. They haven't developed a two way trust with the team and hence they have a hard time, giving instructions and moving away.

What is micro-management?

So what really is micro-management? A manager is micro managing when he gets down to minute details of the project. He wants to be involved in every aspect and wants to be up to date on small scale timelines and expectations. He is essentially displaying lack of trust in the employees. However, new managers need to realize that no employee likes to be micro-managed specially the senior employees. Most people work their best when left alone and empowered to perform their task as they would like to. This is similar to delegation and involves the concept of letting go. If your employees are mature, they will work with you as you make a transition from individual contributor to manager. However, they would also expect you to be ready for the role and demonstrate a level of trust in them.

Why leaders micro-manage?

I personally never micro-managed my teams because I tend to trust people until they give me a reason to distrust them. I have however come across some managers who do micro-manage. Most of the time, they don't trust the employees. These managers think they can do the task better than their employees hence they want to be involved in each and every aspect of the task so they can shape the outcome. These managers like to be in control. If they empower the teams, they would loose control and they would not be comfortable with it. What happens in such cases is these managers are not able to perform actual tasks of a manager such as coaching

8

employees, building trust. They are constantly bogged down by details and trying to keep things under control.

How to avoid micro-management?

Keeping an open door policy helps you to master delegation. You as a manager should give instructions to the team and then empower them to perform their tasks. At the same time, communicate to the team that your doors are open and if they have any doubt or need to discuss the tasks in more detail, they can knock on your door anytime. Be available and be approachable.

The best way to avoid micro-management is to start trusting your employees. Consciously let go of the fear that they will make mistakes. Be comfortable with the notion that if your employees make mistakes, you will be able to handle the scenario in the best possible manner. What you will see is that nine out of ten times, employees will perform very well. They will feel empowered and will take pride in a job well done. Empowering employees has two benefits, one is they feel in control and second, they stop worrying about micro-management. They start trusting their manager more because they feel trusted themselves.

Don't make the mistake of taking the concept of delegation to an extreme. In my entire career, I have come across one manager who took this concept too far. She was completely hands-off and unapproachable. She wouldn't conduct one-on-one meetings, nor discuss goals and timelines. It was only after the fact, you realized that her expectations were different from what you had gathered. This approach leads to chaos, mis-communication, failed expectation and a lot of distrust. Delegation doesn't mean you are completely hands-off. You need to be approachable at the same time.

When micro-management may be necessary?

We have discussed how micro-management leads to distrust. However, some employees do need more guidance than others. The newly graduated employee may not be familiar with the working environment and may need some hand holding. He would need to be mentored by you at least in the beginning and given clear instructions. You also need to check with this employee more often than others and encourage him to ask questions. The key is to distinguish between which employee needs more managing and which needs less. This awareness will help build a stronger team.

There are other exceptions to the rule of delegation. In the case of a problematic employee or under-performing employee a closer watch is required. These employees cannot be treated in the same manner as others and need to be supervised in a different manner. If you are a new manager and you happen to have such an employee in your team, you may want to consult a senior manager, your supervisor or get guidance from the Human Resources department.

Every company has a system in place to help managers deal with difficult or under performing employees. This is not the time to take matters into your hands and think you are a know-it-all. The wiser thing to do is to consult with senior managers and get Human Resources involved from the beginning. Being proactive will avoid a lot of problems in future.

2 NOT GAINING TRUST

Gaining trust is a key quality of a great manager. It is the foundation for every interaction that happens between manager and the employee. You don't want to make the mistake of not gaining trust or having your direct reports distrust you. **This would be a fatal mistake.**

Gaining trust takes time and effort but once it is established, it is very rewarding and makes the team more productive. Sometimes people struggle with the concept of trust. They ask "How do you define trust?" I too struggled with it in the beginning. The best way to describe trust is by giving relevant examples in the context of the relationship involved.

Lets look at some of the ways you can gain trust of your employees.

Provide support when needed

As a manager, you can gain the trust of your employees by taking hurdles and hindrances out of their way. By making their environment as supportive as possible for employees to do their job, trust builds implicitly.

Employees must learn to rely on you as a manager and know that you have their back no matter what. I have had the pleasure of working with some great managers. I still remember one of them distinctly. He was so popular that engineers working in other teams used to enquire with me if he had an opening in his team. They would love to work for him.

You might wonder, what was so good about him? His best quality as a manager was his willingness to stick his neck out to always protect his employees in the face of conflict with another team. He always had our back!

On the contrary, I know a manager who would point out mistakes of his employees in a big crowd. This is a serious mistake leading employees to distrust their manager. In this kind of situation, employees are always on guard; they don't know what the manager might say to put them down. I don't believe this manager criticized his staff to humiliate them; he was simply not self-aware. He didn't see that his actions causing his employees to distrust him.

Another manager I know would not directly point out mistakes his employees' mistakes but would ask employees their opinion of each other. This is a worse mistake because employees talk to each other and sooner or later they will find out that the manager is using them against each other. Such inappropriate discussion leads to distrust and a team can never function productively in such an environment. Why some managers do that is a mystery. I tend to think they are simply not self-aware. These managers are neither aware of the benefits of trust nor the destructive implications of distrust. Trust works two ways, the more you give the more you get.

Enable personal development for career growth via coaching and mentoring.

In order to gain trust a manager should encourage a frank dialogue with the employee for developmental growth. Needless to say, it should be done in a manner so it doesn't come off as criticism but rather as a value add.

A healthy dialogue will help build trust. On the contrary if not done correctly, distrust may be the result. Often managers, when discussing development plans with their employees, point out a weakness and then forget to let go of it. The weakness stays always in the back of their mind and they keep referring to it. The employee believes he is being judged instead of being coached.

Number one rule of thumb for coaching is to point out the weakness and provide suitable environment for employee to learn from his mistakes. Reward his effort to correct the weakness and do not punish every time he errs. Providing a healthy environment for an employee to correct his mistake builds a lifelong trust.

I will share a personal experience. I had a weakness that I struggled with for a number of years. A couple of managers pointed out my weakness but they didn't know how to coach me or provide a healthy environment in which I could improve. They would constantly penalize me for my weakness during annual review but never offered guidance. They expected me to work on it myself and I didn't know how. However after two failed attempts, I finally had the good luck to work for a manager who was a master at coaching. When he discussed my weakness with me, he took it upon himself to healthily help me overcome it!

The element of trust that this manager had developed with me encouraged me to discuss my weakness with him openly. I knew he would not punish me for it. He had the best intention of helping me excel. I would discuss my efforts in improving my weakness with him. I would also discuss my failed attempts. I took advice from him on how to correct it in case I should run into a similar scenario later. It was as if he understood how much I wanted to correct my behavior and that I was struggling with the how-to part. He appreciated my intent to fix the problem and my efforts to fix the weakness. This manager and his coaching had a profound effect on me. I was so happy to realize that dealing with my weakness ultimately led to a new strength in me!

Never micro-manage

No employee likes to be micro-managed. This topic has been discussed in Chapter 1 but it bears repeating. Micro-managing is a fatal mistake for a manager especially in supervising senior employees. Instead focus on how to empower employees. Empowerment leads to productivity and a healthy atmosphere within the team. Micro-managing leads to stress and distrust. Employees are less productive in a micro-managed environment and sooner or later they move on to other jobs.

I know of an incident where an employee was very happy with his job but he didn't like the manager's style because of micro-management. He struggled for a couple of years to stay in the team because he really loved what he was doing. However, the stress of his manager's controlling style got to him after two years and he left the group.

Most micro-managers have a problem with letting go of control. They tend to ask too many questions and follow little details because they cannot trust the employees to figure it out and do their job properly. The distrust shows in their words and actions and it works against them. Employees have a hard time concentrating on the job. They are often stressed by the distrust placed upon them by their manager. Ideally managers are supposed to help employees by taking away their hurdles. **When managers micro-manage, they become the hurdles themselves.**

Reward, reward, and reward

I cannot emphasize enough the importance of rewarding good work. Reward need not always be in the monetary form.

As a manager, you can find creative ways of rewarding employees. Rewarding employees helps build trust. Inadequate rewards or rewarding wrong behaviors develops distrust in the team. Employees often start feeling neglected or overworked when there are inadequate rewards.

One of my managers was very innovative in his ways of rewarding good work. He would offer me a day off as compensatory leave for all the good work I did when I overworked to keep my deadline. His praise for my good work in team meetings was very genuine. His words indicated that he truly understood the amount and quality of effort I had put in to make the deadline. Sometimes, this manager would see that I had an overload of work and he would reward me by taking some things off my plate until I had more time to concentrate on them.

If as a manager, you give more work to people who are performing well and fail to give enough appreciation, sooner or later, they will get discouraged and stop working hard.

Implications of no trust

Lack of trust can lead to serious problems in the team and disrupt a team's productivity. A new manager has a challenge to perform and get the tasks going but they shouldn't neglect the importance of gaining trust. Instead managers should make a conscious effort to gain trust of their employees.

When there is lack of trust, employees have a hard time focusing on the job. They are constantly worried about their future. They are not comfortable and frank with their managers and worried about their job security. I cannot emphasize enough the importance of gaining trust. This is the foundation of the team and should be the number one priority of a manager.

I have seen in my career how lack of trust leads to employees not performing well and in many cases, leaving the group. Trust does take time to build but you can get a head start by not making mistakes that lead to distrust.

3 FOCUSING ON YOUR PERSONAL ACHIEVEMENT

As a manager, considerable responsibility is placed upon you. You have the responsibility of your own conduct, responsibility of your employees and responsibility of leading the team. In all of this undertaking a big no-no is thinking about your personal achievement. The worst mistake a manager can make is be driven by a personal growth agenda. In a perfect team, each team member thinks about team goals. If the manager is driven by personal goals, that would lead to a dysfunctional team.

Why are leaders driven by personal achievement goals?

Have you ever been in a situation where your teammate and you are at odds? You just don't see eye to eye. You are thinking about the team goals and they are thinking they are right! I think we have all been in a situation like this. The crux of this matter is whether a person is driven by personal goals or a team goal.

When people are primarily driven by personal goals, they still achieve things. But whatever they achieve, it is for their own benefit. Sometimes it makes them shine at other people's expense and sometimes it makes them look good at the team's expense. They fail to understand that in the bigger picture, team goals are more important than any individual's achievement. These people are not incompetent. On the contrary, they are highly competitive and they want to win at all costs. What matters to them is they win and they look good.

New managers may tend to make the mistake of being driven by personal achievement since that is what they were used to before becoming managers. As individual contributors, teamwork is required, however in most cases, individuals work independently and are absorbed in their own tasks. It is the task of a good manager to encourage individual contributors to be driven by teamwork.

Personal achievement for a manager can also translate into a manager who is only concerned about whether his team is making its goals, without regard for the larger picture. Even if it is at the expense of another team, what matters to him is that his team looks good. These managers fail to collaborate with other teams or with their peer managers. This kind of thinking can also be transferred to their employees who start thinking about their own personal achievement. Employees may then start working towards their individual tasks at the cost of another team member. The ripple effect continues and destroys the spirit of teamwork.

How to develop team based behavior?

As leaders and managers, we need to lead by example. If we display personal achievement based behavior, we encourage that behavior among our employees. This makes the whole team dysfunctional. When team members only think of personal goals, team goals don't get achieved. Truly speaking the manager of the team is the one to be blamed for this scenario.

Instead of displaying a personal achievement based behavior a good manager recognizes that behavior in others and attempts to correct it by careful coaching. It is not wise for a manager to let an employee be focused on the path of individual achievement no matter how bright the employee is. It is the duty of a good manager to not only encourage team based behavior but also correct the wrong behavior or attitude.

I have seen several examples where an employee is allowed to display personal achievement type behavior because he is technically very good. The manager is afraid to call this out because he is worried he might loose a technically sound individual contributor. The lack of confrontation encourages this behavior and the employee doesn't change. What happens in this case is either other team members leave due to frustration or they become competitive to call attention to themselves. What is worse is when a manager rewards this kind of employee. Rewarding the wrong behavior encourages it.

In one of my peer teams, a technically sound employee was displaying all signs of excessive personal achievement goals. He would want to win at all costs and only be involved in activities that would show him in a good light. Unfortunately his manager couldn't recognize this self-serving approach and kept giving him more opportunities and also promoted him pretty quickly. After his promotion, the employee left for another group within the company. This employee was only driven for personal growth and achievement. His leaving the group was a big loss for the team since he was involved in crucial projects. However, the blame goes to the manager for encouraging and rewarding this employee's wrong behavior.

Advantages of team based achievement

I have observed several instances where teams that displayed teamwork achieved more than others. In most of these cases, the manager was the driving force. The manager displayed through his actions that team goals are above all other goals. What people don't realize is that employees display the behavior that their managers reward. These managers rewarded teamwork all the time. They didn't encourage personal achievement as much as they encouraged teamwork.

I once had an employee in my team who would go out of his way to help his peers. We had set our annual goals and we were all working towards achieving these goals. He saw that one of his peers was struggling with his assigned task. If he didn't get help, our team would be short of achieving the goals we had set for the fiscal year. This employee spoke to me one-on-one and offered to help his peer so our team would be able to meet our goals. I was very impressed by this employee's team spirit. I rewarded him with recognition in the team meeting as well as requested my boss to give him a bonus based on teamwork.

4 NOT GIVING ADEQUATE REWARDS

Rewarding employees is the key to success for a manager. A common mistake managers make not rewarding their employees enough or not rewarding them at appropriate times. They get so busy in managing the team that they forget about recognizing their team's efforts. Rewarding the good work of your employees is crucial to the success of the team. Rewards don't always have to be in monetary form either.

Each employee is motivated differently; Some may be driven by monetary rewards, some by work goals and some by better opportunities or more recognition. Recognizing what drives the employee and giving him that reward is essential to managing an effective team. Avoid the mistake of giving rewards that don't mean a lot to employees. Taking some time to figure out which employee values which kind of reward will go a long way.

Let us look at different forms of rewards a manager can give to his or her employees.

Recognition

If the manager is praising an employee in one-on-one meetings, however fails to praise them in public, this will lead to doubt and distrust. Golden rule of managing employees is – **Praise in public and criticize in private.**

Recognition is a very powerful motivation tool. Recognition can be among peers, among senior managers and customers. One of my managers was very genuine in his praise of his employees. His praise was always heartfelt. Oftentimes, managers make the mistake of going through the motions when praising their employees. They do this as a job, and it shows. The praise doesn't seem genuine. A couple of times, my manager went to a management training and came back and started praising the employees in an unexpected and odd manner. It didn't seem sincere and appeared that he was repeating what he had been told to do. Putting some emotions and thought behind praise and recognition goes a long ways in terms of gaining trust.

Compensatory Time Off

Giving compensatory time off is an effective way to appreciate an employee's hard work and dedication. In some companies, the Human Resources department allow compensatory time off. Even if the Human Resources department doesn't allow it, a good manager can make allowances to give compensatory time off to employees. Similarly allowing flexible schedule in case of family issues is a form of reward. It shows how understanding and accommodating a manager is. You would be surprised how some managers don't seem to value flexibility. They don't realize how it adds to the trust factor. They don't think employees deserve flexibility. These managers have a low emotional intelligence and are making a big mistake by not factoring the human element into their leadership. They may have achieved a lot in their career but they cannot make good managers.

Team Building Activities

Organizing outings and team-building activities is also a healthy way of rewarding employees. This has a dual effect of a better team environment and a productive team. Team members also feel appreciated and get refreshed for the next work day. Allowing the team to choose the team building activities gives them more power. One should choose activities appropriate for the mix of the team members and their interests. Sometimes you don't even need to spend a lot of money to have a good team outing. Once I took my team out hiking in some of the most beautiful surroundings of the San Francisco bay area. It was a treat to see the views and the team had time to bond with each other as well as get invigorated. Check with your Human Resources department on which activities are allowed and then don't hold back on giving your team a good time.

Giving employees increased opportunities

Some employees are more motivated than others. For these employees an opportunity to learn and walk in the shoes of their boss is a rewarding opportunity. Take time to figure out who in your team is more driven and provide them with several growth opportunities. Delegate your own tasks to them and have them attend some of your meetings to give exposure. This would be a moment of pride for them and they will really appreciate your efforts. If there are out-of-ordinary tasks to be performed, give these employees an opportunity to take them. Another common practice in some companies is to allow rotation of jobs for a couple of days or weeks. This would be another way of rewarding the driven employees to have them learn a new skill.

Rewarding good behavior

Rewards need not be given for a job well done; Rewards should also be given for displaying team based behavior. This is a sure way to encourage the right behavior within the team. I have had several employees who went above and beyond to contribute to a team goal and I always made it a point to praise them in team meetings highlighting how their contribution has made a difference in achieving team goals. Often if the manager fails to appreciate a certain behavior and takes it for granted, employees don't get the sense if they are indeed on the right path. Don't take good behavior for granted, appreciate it and encourage it. This has two advantages, you are building trust with the employee as well as encouraging the right behavior within the team. Soon, other employees will start exhibiting similar behavior.

5 RUNNING FROM CONFLICTS

Conflicts are part of work life. As a leader, you will run into more conflicts than otherwise. This is natural because you are dealing with more people. People have different opinions and the more people you deal with the more chances you will run into opposing views. Don't make the mistake of fleeing conflicts. Rather learn to deal with them. You need to be strong to deal with conflicts.

Before stepping into a leadership role, ask yourself if you can deal with conflicts effectively or not? If not, perhaps taking a course on conflict management is a good idea. One cannot avoid conflicts when working with other people and one should learn how to deal with them. **This is a crucial skill a manager needs to have.**

Lets take a look at various scenarios a manager can run into which might cause conflicts with other co-workers.

Dealing with difficult employees

Every leader in his or her career has dealt with one or more difficult employees. New managers may not be looking forward to it but sooner or later they will have to learn the skill of managing difficult employees.

The foremost question to ask is why are some employees difficult?

I believe there are two kinds of difficult employees

- Disgruntled or frustrated employees sometimes become difficult employees.

- Some employees are plain difficult (may have been bullies growing up)

The art of managing difficult employees is to recognize which of these categories you are dealing with. The solution of how to manage them will completely depend on your assessment. Disgruntled employees for example need to be dealt with lot of care. They need reassurance that their frustration will be taken care of. These employees became disgruntled because of some bad experience in their past. They will not change overnight but when dealt with properly, these employees can be managed to become productive. Genuinely try to understand where their frustration is coming from and assure them that the past experience in indeed past and they don't need to worry about it anymore. One of the engineers I hired had previously been misjudged by her manager. Her efforts were not adequately appreciated in the past and she had become quite disgruntled about it. She implicitly expected me to do the same. I sensed this and made extra effort to appreciate her good work and gave her more opportunities to exhibit her technical skills. Slowly she started to see that I was different from her previous manager and we developed a trust between us.

Dealing with bullies is a completely different strategy. You need to be stronger to deal with these employees and let them know they cannot be bullies any more, this is not high school and that a certain behavior is expected of them as adults. They turned into bullies because no one told them what they were doing was wrong. I worked with an employee who was technically strong but who had a temper. Whenever his peers made a mistake, he would start abusing them. After getting some complaints about him, I decided to have a frank conversation with him. At first, he didn't want to admit his wrong behavior but I gave him some concrete examples, I showed him some emails he had written to other team members. He then admitted that he indeed had a weakness of abusing people if they were in the wrong. He said he also exhibited this behavior at home but he would try and work on improving it. In our subsequent one-on-one meetings, we would discuss this behavior and how he is working on improving it. It took sometime but eventually he was able to control his temper and become more tactful about giving feedback to his peers.

Supervising either bullies or disgruntled employees is not an easy task but understanding which behavior you are dealing with will make it easier to handle.

Conducting Performance Evaluations

Most managers (if not all) dread when the time comes to give performance evaluations to their employees. This begs the question why? Employee evaluation should not be such a fearful process. After all, aren't managers also supposed to be coaches? Isn't this the time for employee growth and development? Shouldn't performance evaluation be the time where managers can be proud of their coaching skills?

Well, there is only one explanation of why this happens. These managers don't give the direct feedback to the employees all year round and wait for the annual performance evaluation to have the discussion. Talking about an employee's performance evaluation only once a year is not the way to go about it. Some companies have started doing mid-year review. Even if companies don't mandate a mid-year performance evaluation, managers should make it a habit to give feedback to the employee throughout the course of the working year.

The feedback should not come as a surprise to the employee at the performance evaluation time. If your feedback to an employee is going to be a surprise, that would certainly make the process difficult and something to dread. In reality, coaching employees is one of the most rewarding skills for a manager and your goal should be to make it work for both you and your employees. If trust has already been developed between manager and employee, having this discussion is much easier and more productive.

Difficult conversation with your supervisor

No matter how good your relationship with your boss is, when you are in a leadership position, there will be times where your opinion and/or decision will differ from that of your supervisor. Having that difficult conversation with your boss is a tricky situation to handle.

As a general rule, in business it is taught that the boss is always right. So then how do you tell them that you think otherwise? Well, it is simple, much like any other confrontation, you need to be able to get in their shoes. Try and understand why they are taking the stand they are taking. How can you reason with them that there is a flaw in their thinking? Make it a logical discussion rather than emotional. Ensure that you are not hurting anyone's ego and respect the boss-subordinate relationship, while still standing up for your opinions.

I was not shy of having these discussions with my supervisor in my earlier years of leadership career. However I made the mistake of not honoring the boss-subordinate relationship in the manner I should have. There is a way to make your voice heard without going the aggressive path especially when delicate relationships are involved. I was too hot headed at times to realize that my behavior was not honoring the boss-subordinate relationship.

How to deal with conflicts

Conflict management is a crucial skill required for all managers. It is best to learn conflict management skills before taking on a role of a manager. Do you often find yourself avoiding conflicts because of the fear involved? Well, you may be suffering from conflict phobia. And it's probably time to overcome that phobia and turn fear into a strength. The key to dealing with any conflict is to act like a true winner. And to do this is to look for a win-win outcome for everyone involved.

Conflicts occur when people have differing opinions or different ways of doing things. Conflicts are inevitable because, by nature people are different and work in different ways. We often come from different backgrounds and cultures and our thinking often varies, too.

People who have strong opinions tend to get into observable conflicts with their counterparts more often than others do. Or, said another way, certain people are "pre-wired" to engage in conflict and, upon observation, it will be overt and obvious to us when they do.

Why people engage in conflicts

- One reason is that these determined people are actually energized by the process of engaging in conflict. They actually like it (...think boxer...)! Or, perhaps, they value expediency and see that a quick and overt confrontation is a means to a quick and conclusive end to the dissonant discourse.
- Conversely, people on the other end of the conflict-engagement-spectrum may tend to avoid conflict at all cost because it requires so much energy, effort, and emotional toil. To them, the perceived battle just isn't worth the engagement.

Engaging in conflict isn't necessarily a negative thing. Nor is it a bad thing, since it is good to have opinions. But the ones who stand their ground quickly, overtly, and vocally can give conflict a bad name. Most people approach a conflict with an egoistic view and believe they have to win. But unfortunately, this is a mistake.

The first thing to keep in mind is that it is okay to be in a conflict. But you need to be able to handle escalating conflict in the right way. Going into a conflict with the mindset that *"I have to find a win-win situation for both parties"* always results in a good outcome because your intention is right. By doing this, you have set a goal for a win-win scenario.

So the question now is *"How does one find that win-win outcome?"* Well, the answer comes when you finds the way to step into the opponent's shoes and try to think like they do. Or the next best situation is to try to figure out why the opponent is acting in a certain way; or asking yourself what is it that they are looking to resolve in the conflicting situation.

Working outside of your own perceptions and launching into the realm of solutions obtainable by both parties is the key to figuring out a win-win outcome. Once you have analyzed the situation from both your perspective and your opponents' perspective, you will certainly think of a win-win outcome. Be open when resolving a conflict with the other party; this open attitude is the key to a successful resolution.

Once you have made the (oftentimes uncomfortable) decision to yield your own will to that of a higher position of an empathetic outcome, you will find yourself in fresh territory that is void of negative dissonance. You will find it is easier to compromise and bury the hatchet with your enemy.

You are now ready to discuss the win-win outcome with the person you previously thought of as your opponent. When the other party hears what you have to say as it is couched in empathetic, honorable terms, he or she will automatically soften their tone and perspective and be willing to work with you. Note that the final outcome may or may not be different from what you suggested, but as long as it is a win-win, you should be able to accept it.

This means that when you are negotiating a win-win outcome with the other party, you need to be open-minded about it. You don't want to appear rigid and have an obstinate mindset that appears that you are thinking what you suggested is the best, and the only, possible outcome.

So, the next time you see a conflict in the workplace :
  1. Don't flee it!
  2. Don't be afraid to tackle it!
  3. Instead, go for a concise and honorable resolution!

Once you have handled it, you will value how easy it feels and how accomplished you feel coming out of the conflict.

6 NOT COACHING EMPLOYEES

Coaching and developing employees is one of the most rewarding aspect of a manager's job. You should not shy away from it. Given the increased number of responsibilities that a new manager has, this aspect may be pushed down the stack and not given enough importance. Coaching is a win-win for both the manager and the employees. Many new managers neglect the coaching role in the beginning or have not yet developed this muscle. I encourage you to take time out to develop and coach your employees.

Some managers make the mistake of coaching employees only once a year as required by the company's Human Resources department typically during annual review. However if a manager only does this task once a year, that is worse than not doing it at all. Coaching ideally is an ongoing process where the manager and employee sit down and discuss the employee's strengths and weaknesses, employee's career aspirations, development plan and other relevant topics. Later, they track progress and the manager provides guidance to help the employee succeed in his or her defined goals.

Coaching and developing of employees can be on a technical or soft skills level or it may be behavioral or for any other aspirations the employee might have. The key is to have the conversation meaningfully and to keep track of how the employee is performing with respect to the goals set by the manager and the employee.

Developing an employee has several benefits. It is good overall for the company. It is definitely improving the employee's career and at the same time building trust between manager and employee. This task also provides the manager an opportunity to do succession planning. Succession planning is often neglected in companies. It is done for very senior positions only but not so much for first level managers.

Lets look at opportunities for a manager to coach and develop employees.

Resolving conflicts between employees

As a manager, I have often encountered situations where employees didn't see eye to eye. I was initially amazed at the behavior since these are mature educated adults we are dealing with and yet, they were at odds with each other for one reason or another.

One way to handle this problem is to let the employees deal and resolve it amongst themselves. However, sometimes it leads to a not so productive environment in the team and the manager needs to interfere and resolve the situation. One mistake you don't want to make is to take sides. You ought to come out as a fair manager no matter what the situation is. Employees have their own perspective on the situations. You can bring some objectivity into the situation.

It works in a manager's favor is when he deals with the situation effectively and is see to have dealt with it fairly. Also, it is timely to coach the employees who are in disagreement such that if a similar situation appears in the future, they would be able to resolve it among themselves.

Helping staff overcome their weaknesses

Another excellent opportunity to coach employees is through the review cycle and performance evaluations. Take this time, to really help the employee in both technical as well as behavioral aspects. This is the most rewarding aspect of being a manager and everyone should make use of it.

When managers fail to do this aspect of their job effectively, they loose out on the opportunity to build rapport with their employees. Having the opportunity to develop an employee is by far the best way to build an everlasting trust with them. Of all the leaders I have worked with, I remember most clearly the ones who taught me skills for life. They took time to coach and develop me and got my attention, respect and trust.

This is not an easy task, as it takes time to observe and listen to the employee. You need to have the right conversation with them in order to understand the weakness and its root cause. Most importantly, you need to have built some amount of trust with the employee for them to open up with you.

Succession planning

Another opportunity to coach employees is when you are strategizing and planning for a successor to yourself. This is probably the best way to coach an employee. You can tag them along with you and have them learn by observation or delegate some of your own tasks to them. You can ask them to attend some of your meetings on your behalf. They will learn by making their own mistakes but they will honor the opportunity to walk in your shoes.

I have had the pleasure of working with a great leader who gave me the responsibility of performing his tasks as well as representing him in senior leadership meetings. This gave me the exposure as well as responsibility to learn at the same time. I also respected him as a leader since he was very secure in himself and allowed me to step in his shoes and learn. This is the best way to learn how to do the job of next level.

Build the culture of coaching

Whether your company supports a culture of coaching or not, as a manager, you can certainly advocate and develop this culture within your team. Encourage your senior employees to coach junior employees. Reward the employees who are displaying mentoring and coaching skills. Don't take their coaching behavior for granted, appreciate it, encourage it and reward it. You can encourage your employees to look for mentors outside of your team especially if they would like to pursue a different role in the future. Needless to say, some amount of trust is necessary for this kind of culture to flourish.

Some companies offer employees the opportunity to work with independent executive coaches. This is another way of rewarding high potential employees. However I feel the very best way to learn is by emulating someone in your field, by watching them and learn ing from their actions. This calls for us as managers to lead by example. Sometimes employees learn even by subtly observing you as a leader.

7 NOT BUILDING INTERPERSONAL RELATIONSHIPS

Interpersonal relationships are key for a leader or manager to succeed in the business world. Without these relationships, she will not be able to achieve much nor will she have a successful team.

As a leader, you don't want to make the mistake of not building interpersonal relationships. Who will you have to make these relationships with? Pretty much everyone you work with, your direct reports, your peers, your supervisors and senior managers as well as administrative assistants. These relationships will make your job easier for you. Lack of relationships will make the job harder. When individual contributors are promoted from within the team to the role of a manager, cultivating interpersonal relationships may be a new skill to them. They are used to performing by themselves and take pride in doing their job by themselves. As a manager, the opposite is true, you can only do so much yourself. Relationship skills are very important and new managers should be consciously developing this tool.

Let's take a look at some of these relationships and their different aspects in detail.

Relationship with peers

As an individual contributor, relationships are important but not as important as when you are functioning as a manager. As a manager you are not only representing yourself but representing the whole team.

As you accept more responsibility, you can also use positive relationships in achieving more for the team. Having a good relationship with peer managers is very essential for the success of a team. You need to cultivate a culture of collaboration and teamwork not only within your team but also across teams. If your relationship with peer managers is good, it leads to better collaboration between teams. This spirit of cooperation also ensures that if a situation arises where there is conflict between two teams, it can be resolved in a better manner.

When I took on the role of a software development manager, I soon realized that I not only needed to develop a good relationship with other development managers but also with test managers. Test managers were more willing to take a small hit in schedule if I had a favorable relationship with them. When I didn't have a good relationship with the test managers, even a small mistake from my team would be highlighted and not tolerated. Similarly a good relationship with program managers and product managers was necessary to get the product development done in time and according to customer requirements. In cases of customer problems, a good relationship with account managers and the customer support department was very essential for success. A good communication with account managers ensured that all information flow was done in time between engineering teams and the customers and that nothing was lost in translation. It also helped relieve some of the pressure in a stressful situation of a high priority customer problem.

As a manager, your visibility increases tenfold and so does your responsibility. Good inter personal relationship makes the job much easier. You cannot achieve much by going alone!

Relationship with supervisors

The most important and most delicate relationship you have as a manager is with your supervisor.

I would say if you have to master one relationship before taking up the role of a manager, master this one!

Why is this relationship delicate? It requires a balance between exerting your decision making power and yielding to your boss when required. The key to success in this relationship is to learn that balance. It is important to learn in which situations you want to exert your opinion and in which situation, you need to yield.

When I took the role of a manager, I made the mistake of not realizing this balance. I tended to exert more of my own opinions. On the other hand, if a new manager is not assertive enough she is not considered strong or capable. You certainly want to learn how to balance it.

One rule of thumb is never make your boss look bad, no matter what! That would be a fatal mistake specially if your boss looks bad in front of his seniors. That situation would not go well for anyone.

Relationship with direct reports

A good relationship with direct reports is also very important for success both for you as a manager and for your team. When your direct reports look up to you as a leader, it is a very rewarding feeling.

You need to be their coach, friend, guide and a trustworthy partner. There are many opportunities to develop this relationship including providing rewards for a job well done, coaching and developing them in their career, and team building activities. As a manager, this was my favorite part of the job, to be able to have a good relationship with all my direct reports. You want to keep an open door policy with each and every employee and listen to their problems and be as supportive as you can be.

Relationship with vendors/recruiters

As a manager, you will be dealing with vendors and keeping a good relationship with them will help you get access to current technology and resources needed for your team to succeed. Another important relationship is the one you will build with recruiters. Recruiters can help you to hire the right talent.

Professional recruiters spent time short-listing candidates and will help you pick the right person for your team.

Relationship with customers

A customer centric approach is the best approach for an organization. Managers also have to deal with customers, sometimes in not so welcome scenarios.

If customers run into problems with the product, a good relationship helps smooth the rough edges and allows you to work on problems in a more constructive manner.

Implications of lack of interpersonal relationships

Relationships are so important for a manager that lack of crucial relationship can bring his entire empire down. Managers are assessed for their performance not only on the basis of team goals being achieved but also on interpersonal relationships. When managers get 360 degree feedback from their peers and seniors, lack of interpersonal relationships will get highlighted. There are other ways in which this can hurt the manager and his team. Other managers may perceive this manager as snobbish. They may not collaborate well with him and his teams. The human element should never be neglected. Human beings are social creatures and a lot gets done in a friendly environment. A leader also learns more if he works cooperatively with others. He learns from other managers and their experience, and together they help each other. Don't make the mistake of shying away from relationships. Instead make an extra effort to build the critical relationships you and your team will need in order to succeed.

How to develop healthy relationships

Healthy relationships are important for a manager to succeed at his job; I can't say that too many times. A multitude of relationships must be formed and maintained over time if you are to attain success, so it is important to master this skill early in your career. Building healthy relationships should become part of a manager's lifestyle such that he is using this skill unconsciously. Strong, mutually rewarding relationships are all about give and take. Once you become a master at relationships, you will realize that neither party is as important as the relationship itself. If one has to yield in some circumstances to maintain a healthy relationship, then one should do that. Always look for a win-win outcome in relationships.

8 NOT LISTENING TO PEOPLE YOU MANAGE

We all aspire to be motivating and exemplary leaders. Some are born leaders, some learn the tricks of the trade on the job and there are some who are always learning and getting better. Haven't you often wondered what is the most sought after leadership quality? There are of course many qualities a great leader needs to have but there has got to be one gem.

In my mind, **great leaders are those who listen to their people**. As a manager, it is fatal to make the mistake of not listening to the voice of your team. When you don't take their input into consideration, you develop a wall of distrust between you and your team.

You as a manager obviously have the decision making power and skills. Before you make your decisions, you need to listen to your people. Listening is a tricky art, there are some managers who listen but don't comprehend. There are some managers who listen but cannot convey it back to their people that they have listened and are now acting on the feedback. And there are some managers who think, while they are listening, on how to respond to comments because they are not truly listening!

Think for a moment and ensure that you are not one of those managers who do not truly listen to their people. Listening to your staff members and understanding their perspective is a great leadership tool. If you give your attention to the problems they are facing and decide to act on those problems in a practical way, it can go a very long way in establishing yourself as a true leader. Even if there is no clear solution in sight, simply communicating that you have heard the problem, is a good start. When employees feel they have been heard, it puts their mind at rest, makes them more productive, and most of all, it makes them respect their leaders.

Ways to listen better

A great listening tool for managers is 360 degree feedback which allows managers to get anonymous feedback from their co-workers, direct reports, supervisors etc. Getting the feedback and acting on it plus sharing that information with your direct reports is also a good way of building trust with your team. Conducting a 360 degree feedback session is essential for new managers. Getting feedback is also a good tool to use if you are a seasoned manager but have changed jobs and are now managing a new team.

I still remember in one of my 360 degree feedback session, I got a comment that "She mostly does all the work herself and doesn't give us the opportunity to help her out". In some ways it was a complement on my capacity to do more but on the other hand I realized that in my zeal to accomplish a lot, I was not giving enough opportunities to my employees. At that point of time, I had taken on two roles in my organization so I had a lot of responsibility on my shoulders. I could have off-loaded some of it by involving my employees in the extra project. I was thinking that it was my initiative and perhaps they would not be interested in participating. But after receiving that feedback, I realized they were indeed curious and eager to participate in the extra project. I therefore started involving my employees and it brought a more healthy exchange of ideas to the table.

There was another scenario in which my team and my seniors held differing viewpoints. I had heard both viewpoints and having contemplated the issues at length, I decided to go with the opinion of my seniors – not because it was my seniors' viewpoint but because I thought it was more appropriate. The problem was that I never communicated back to my team why I went with the seniors' opinion. They were starting to distrust me until one employee asked me the reason for my decision. I immediately realized I had failed to communicate the reasons for my decision. I had not shared with my team the process I used to come to my decision. I immediately corrected the issue and after I explained the reasoning, they were able to come to terms with it. Two-way communication is essential between managers and the employees.

9 HAVING AN EGO

One of my colleagues rightfully said, "**Check your ego at the door when stepping into a leadership position!**" Ego can be your worst enemy when you are performing as a leader or a manager. Ego is one of the hardest thing to deal with, but one has to be able to put ego aside when managing a team. This is somewhat related to the subject of team goals versus personal goals as discussed in chapter 3. Quite often you will find that seasoned managers are free of ego issues because they have already worked on releasing their false pride.

Implications of a leader with an ego

An inflated ego can have a harmful effect on your behavior. The number one quality a leader needs to have is good listening skills, and ego gets in the way of listening. When you cannot put your ego aside, you may hear what your employees are telling you but you will not listen openly to them. This is especially true when what they are telling you is against what you are thinking. Number one rule for a manager is that team comes before self.

Managers with ego issues fail to listen to their employees and do what they think is right. This kind of thinking may work for them in the short term but it fails in the long run. Employees distrust these managers or fail to respect them. They may even stop giving useful feedback to these managers because they can see it is not going to be heard.

Why leaders have ego issues

There could be several reasons why someone would have an inflated ego. I tend to think the person who is acting out of ego knows inside his heart that he should be acting otherwise. His ego holds this leader back from doing the right thing. What he fails to comprehend is that leaders are constantly being followed, watched, and observed. When you act out of ego as a leader, it goes against you and only gains for you less respect and some amount of distrust. It is also a sign of an immature leader.

If a leader is used to people always agreeing to what they propose, he or she tends to develop a false sense of always being right. This type of leader has a hard time dealing with someone who has opposing views. Ego comes from insecurity and not being comfortable with listening to a different point of view. Sometimes a leader develops a false ego if there is no competitor. Without competition they develop a false sense of being really good and always being right. They start thinking they have lots of power and see no need to listen to others.

How to overcome ego issues

If you are struggling with ego issues, detach yourself from the scenario. Observe the situation as a third person and then observe your behavior and figure what out what is wrong with the picture. This detachment is not easy to do, especially when your own behavior has been sub-optimal. However, this is an extremely effective method of dealing with ego issues and leads to better decision making.

Another effective technique to deal with ego issues is to confide in a trusted friend. Ask this person to observe you objectively and give you honest feedback when they see you acting out of ego. This simple tactic can be extremely helpful and will help you make changes faster.

Having said that, oftentimes managers find themselves in situations where they have to act quickly and they might make ego-driven mistakes. In such cases, admit that you have made a mistake. Acknowledging your weakness and correcting it is the best way to gain trust and respect as a leader. As human beings, we all have both strengths and weaknesses. Don't be afraid to acknowledge your weakness and set an intent to work on fixing it. Being in a denial mode and not admitting your mistake is going to work against you. Others will perceive you as immature and will not be able to trust you completely.

10 NOT BEING SELF-AWARE

An understanding of emotional intelligence is the best thing that has happened to explaining leadership in a long time. Leadership skills were a mystery until Daniel Goleman introduced the concept of emotional intelligence in his book titled "Emotional Intelligence : Why It Can Matter More Than IQ". A good manager is one with a balanced mix of technical skills as well as emotional intelligence. Oftentimes, we see technically perfect individuals being promoted to the role of a manager within a team but then failing to excel at management. The reason behind their failure is their low or under-developed emotional intelligence.

What is emotional intelligence?

To be emotionally intelligent is to be aware of your own emotions as well as those of individuals you are dealing with. Most people are quite good at understanding others' emotions but they have a hard time getting a grasp on their own emotions. Being aware of your own feelings and emotional responses is very important for a leader. An emotionally intelligent person is able to not only understand his emotions but is also able to control his emotional responses.

What is Self-Awareness?

There are several components of emotional intelligence. My favorite emotional intelligence aspect is Self-awareness. Self awareness is the hardest of all aspects to develop. I wouldn't think anyone is born with self awareness but how and when they acquire it can make a big difference in their lives. As a manager, this quality can be extremely useful and can make one a very effective leader. This is also a crucial quality for a manager to have in order to succeed. Lack of self-awareness will really limit the reach of a leader.

Unfortunately, when I took the role of a manager, I wasn't as self-aware as I would have liked to be. I wouldn't blame anyone or any circumstance for it. As a manager I ran into scenarios that I had not experienced before and hence I was not aware of how I would react in those circumstances. Some of these circumstances were not favorable. I learned a lot about myself and became more self-aware.

Advantages of Self-Awareness

There are many ways managers can use self awareness to their advantage. As a leader, if you are self-aware, you know your strengths and weakness very well. When you are assembling a team, you want to hire people with complementary strengths to yours. This way you can build a stronger team and get the work done most effectively. However, you should be able to be comfortable in your skin and realize that people you are hiring are better than you in certain areas. New managers have a hard time dealing with this aspect and tend to hire people with similar strengths. This conservative stance is not productive as they can never develop complementary skills in the team.

Self-awareness also teaches us that no one is perfect. We all have our unique strengths and weaknesses. Those seeking perfection in themselves or others will soon realize that it is not a quality they should be looking for when hiring people. Knowing that no one is perfect allows leaders to be less self critical and more productive.

Another way self-awareness works for you as a leader is it makes you more open to taking feedback and/or criticism in a healthy way. Without self-awareness, one tends to be defensive and cannot accept feedback in stride. Accepting feedback is the key to improving yourself. Accepting feedback is also a very important part of the job of a manager. As a manager you can constantly working with people. You are surrounded by peer managers, program and product managers, your employees, and your seniors. Imagine the amount of feedback you will get as a manager! It is ten fold the feedback you got as an individual contributor. Listening to this feedback, accepting it, and embracing it as a tool to help you become more self-aware is the key to becoming a better manager!

How to become more self-aware

In order to become more self-aware, you first need to be open and honest about yourself. You need to be able to identify and accept your weaknesses. Most weaknesses can be overcome. Some take more time than others. However the key is to be open about learning about yourself and your emotions. This is not an easy thing to do. If you are having difficulty with this goal and becoming discouraged, think long-term. By working to overcome any personal weaknesses you identify, you are going to benefit for many years to come.. Your current leadership state may be good enough but in order to become better, self-awareness is a must.

ABOUT THE AUTHOR

Aditi Chopra is a motivating leader, process consultant and a creative writer. She utilizes her experience in software engineering, people management and communication strategies to help create value for organizations.

www.ingramcontent.com/pod-product-compliance
Lightning Source LLC
Chambersburg PA
CBHW071646170526
45166CB00003B/1449